Vic Reeves

James Roderick Moir, born on 24th January 1959, Leeds, West Riding of Yorkshire, England, UK, better known by his stage name **Vic Reeves**, is a comedian, artist, musician, actor and TV presenter, best known for his double act with Bob Mortimer as 'Vic and Bob,' along with his surreal sense of humour. Reeves and Mortimer were listed in The Observer as one of the 50 funniest acts in British comedy during 2003. In a poll to find the Comedians' Comedian in 2005, Vic and Bob were voted as the 8th-greatest comedy act ever by fellow comedians and comedy insiders.

James took an apprenticeship in mechanical engineering at a factory in Newton Aycliffe after leaving school, before later moving to London. He also formed the Fashionable Five, a group of 5 friends, including Jack Dent, who ran the original Fan Club, who'd follow bands including the Enid and Free onto stage, performing pranks, like Moir pretending to have a brass hand, also following a Terry Scott lookalike around Darlington town centre in single-file formation. They later formed their own group, James having an early breakthrough with the help of comedian Malcolm Hardee.

He began a part-time course at a local art college during 1983, developing his liking for painting, persuading a local art gallery to stage an exhibition of his work. Although still best known as a comedian, Moir has a growing a reputation as an artist, his drawings and paintings having been used on his TV shows, forming a large part of his book, Sun Boiled Onions (1999).

As well as working and performing in bands in London, including being an original member of the Industrial/Experimental group 'Test Dept', going onstage with them at their debut gig then leaving soon afterwards, James joined the alternative comedy circuit under many different guises. These included a loudmouthed American called Jim Bell, a beat poet named Mister Mystery then 'The North-East's Top Light Entertainer'— Vic Reeves.

His stage show Vic Reeves Big Night Out began as a regular Thursday night gig at Goldsmith's Tavern, New Cross, later the New Cross House. There, he met Bob Mortimer, a solicitor who attended the show, enjoying it so much that he soon began to take part. Moir's TV début was in December 1986 on Channel 4's 'The Tube', in a comedy game show segment called Square Celebrities, being suspended by a wire to ask the 'celebrities' questions.

His next appearance was on the short-lived chat/comedy show 'One Hour with Jonathan Ross', in a game show segment known as Knock Down Ginger. James's growing TV profile led to Big Night Out being given a slot on Channel 4 the following year, as he and Mortimer rented a back room at Jools Holland's office/recording studio in Westcombe Park, Greenwich where they'd spend hours writing material.

Moir chose the stage name Reeves because of his fondness for the American singer Jim Reeves. He continued to work alongside Mortimer as a comedy duo in The Smell of Reeves and Mortimer, Shooting Stars, and 'Bang Bang, It's Reeves and Mortimer', some of which also featured future cast members of The Fast Show and Little Britain.

James is one of the few comedians to have had a UK chart-topping single, with The Wonder Stuff, singing 'Dizzy', previously a # 1 for Tommy Roe. Moir also released two other singles from

2

his album I Will Cure You (1991). A pilot programme written by Paul Whitehouse and Charlie Higson during 1994, entitled The Honeymoon's Over, was due to feature Chris Bell, a character from The Smell of Reeves and Mortimer but the series was never commissioned. That same year, Vic made a guest appearance on the Radio 1 series Shuttleworth's Showtime, hosted by John Shuttleworth.

James and Bob presented the Channel X produced BBC Saturday game show 'Families at War' with Alice Beer from August 1998 and May 1999. Moir played Marty Hopkirk in the BBC's thriller series Randall and Hopkirk (Deceased) between 2000–2001—a revival of the original series from the 1960s, with Mortimer as Randall, Emilia Fox as Jeannie and Tom Baker as Wyvern.

James presented a series entitled, Vic Reeves Examines on UK Play in the year 2000, featuring celebrities including Ricky Gervais, Johnny Vegas, Lauren Laverne and Emma Kennedy discussing a topic of their choice. That same year, Moir presented a one-off radio show on BBC Radio 1, entitled Cock of the Wood. Reeves appeared on the BBC Radio programme Desert Island Discs during 2003.

James and his 2nd wife, Nancy Sorrell were both contestants on the 4th series of I'm a Celebrity... Get Me Out of Here! the following year. Moir was then featured in the series Catterick with Mortimer, appearing as several characters. He hosted a show for Virgin Radio in September 2005, titled Vic Reeves Big Night In, produced by Mark Augustyn, for a short period on Wednesdays & Thursdays from 7.00pm.

James presented a programme on ITV Tyne Tees during May the following year, about Northeast comedy culture, named It's Funny Up North with... Vic Reeves. Moir presented an historical

3

10-part series, entitled Rogues Gallery, shown on the Discovery Channel (UK) in 2005, in which he investigated, and portrayed Anne Bonny, Mary Read, Captain Kidd, Claude Duval, Jonathan Wild, Rob Roy, Colonel Blood, George Ransley, Deacon Brodie, Blackbeard and Dick Turpin, Nancy Sorrell appearing in some episodes. Vic Reeves' Pirates was shown on ITV West then on the History Channel during 2007.

James also hosted a show titled 'Vic Reeves Investigates: Jack the Ripper', in which he tried to discover who Jack the Ripper was, with the help of historians and leading experts. At the end of the show, Moir came to the conclusion that Jack the Ripper was Francis Tumblety. Vic was the main presenter of Brainiac: Science Abuse from 8th May 2007, during the 5th & 6th series, replacing Richard Hammond. Reeves presented a BBC Radio 2 panel game show titled Does the Team Think? from June that year.

James appeared in a weekly sketch show on BBC Radio 2 from 17th November 2007, entitled Vic Reeves' House Arrest. The show's premise was that Moir had been put under house arrest for 'a crime he didn't commit', each episode being comprised of the events that took place in and around his house on a particular day. Bob played his housecall-making hairdresser, Carl, while other performers included The Mighty Boosh star Noel Fielding as a local vagrant who came to Vic's door on a weekly basis looking for work, as well as Sorrell in multiple roles.

James announced on 27th February 2008 that he and Mortimer were working together on a new sitcom about super heroes who got their powers via a malfunctioning telegraph pole, having also reiterated his desire to bring back Shooting Stars for a 6th series. Along with his son, Reeves was also featured an edition of a factual series for Five, Dangerous Adventures for Boys, based on the best-selling book of that name by Conn and Hal Iggulden.

Moir appeared as presenter of the first episode of My Brilliant Britain in February 2009, one of the new shows commissioned for UKTV People channel's relaunch as Blighty. Vic appeared as a guest on the BBC One's The One Show with Bob on 25th August 2009, the day before Series 6 of Shooting Stars began, featuring James and Mortimer, along with Ulrika Jonsson and Jack Dee as team captains.

Reeves appeared as one of the guests in Reece Shearsmith's Haunted House that autumn, a light-hearted radio discussion show broadcast on BBC Radio 4 in two parts either side of Halloween, on 29th October then 5th November. Moir also voiced a Virgin Atlantic Airlines onboard safety video, with Dani Behr. Vic & Bob performed a selection of YouTube improvised comedy sketches during July 2011, in association with Foster's, posting their 'Afternoon Delight' clips every weekday afternoon that month.

James has appeared without Mortimer on a number of British TV shows, mainly game shows, poll programmes and charity telethons, including:

Year(s)	Title	Channel	Role	No. of episodes	Notes
2017	Coronation Street	ITV	Colin Callen	7+	Credited as Jim Moir
2017	Celebrity Masterchef	BBC 1	Contestant		

2015   Catchphrase: Celebrity Couples Special   ITV
Contestant   1

With Bob Mortimer

Celebrity Benchmark   Channel 4
       Benchmarker/contestant

Celebrity Fifteen to One Channel 4   Contestant   1

Room 101   BBC 1   1

Inspector George Gently   BBC 1   Geoffrey Episode
7.3 'Gently Among Friends'   credited as Jim Moir

2014

Tipping Point: Lucky Stars   ITV   Contestant   1
Won   credited as Jim Moir

Racing Legends: Barry Sheene   BBC 2   Presenter 1

credited as Jim Moir

2013

Big Star's Little Star   ITV Contestant   1   with
daughters Nell and Lizzie (2nd October), credited as Jim Moir

2013

Great British Menu   BBC 2   Guest judge   1
credited as Jim Moir

2012

Hebburn   BBC 2   Joe Pearson   5   credited
as Jim Moir

2012

The Million Pound Drop Channel 4   Contestant – with Bob
Mortimer   1

credited as Jim Moir

2012

The Ministry of Curious Stuff   CBBC   Presenter (with
Dan Skinner)   13

credited as Jim Moir

2011

Vic Reeves' Turner Prize Moments   Channel 4
          Presenter   1

The Fun Police Channel 4   Richard Traves 1   Pilot
credited as Jim Moir

Eric and Ernie   BBC 2 George Bartholomew, father of Eric
Morecambe   1

credited as Jim Moir

2010

Never Mind The Buzzcocks   BBC 2   Panelist – on
Noel Fielding's team   1

Series 24   Episode 9

2009

My Brilliant Britain   Blighty presenter   1   2008

Celebrity Come Dine With Me   Channel 4   waiter / support
for contestant Nancy Sorrell   1

Dangerous Adventures For Boys Five   Contestant (with son,
Louis Moir)   1

Hole in the Wall BBC 1   Contestant (with Nancy Sorrell)
1

The Culture Show Uncut   BBC 2   Reporter   1

Take It Or Leave It   Challenge   Celebrity contestant
(with Nancy Sorrell)   1

2008 BRIT Awards   ITV   Award presenter

2007–2008

Would I Lie To You?   BBC 1   Panel member   2

2005–2008

8 Out of 10 Cats Channel 4   Panel member   8

2007

Loose Women   ITV Interviewee (with Nancy Sorrell)
        1

The One Show   BBC 1   Interviewee 1

Something for the Weekend   BBC 2   Interviewee
1

Deadline   ITV2   Contestant (with Nancy Sorrell)
1

Memoirs of a Cigarette Channel 4   Contributor   1

Vic Reeves' Pirates	HTV the History Channel
	Presenter	6

Vic Reeves Investigates: Jack the Ripper Sky One
	Presenter

Pirate Ship... Live	Five	Presenter

The Big Fat Anniversary Quiz	Channel 4	Guest appearance

Brainiac: Science Abuse Sky One	Presenter	21
Series 5 & 6

Shaun the Sheep	CBBC	BBC 1	Theme tune 'Shaun the Sheep – Life's a Treat'

Vernon Kay's Gameshow Marathon	ITV1	Panel member
1	Blankety Blank episode

100 Greatest Stand Ups Channel 4	Contributor

The Grumpy Guide to... Art	BBC 2	Contributor
	Spinoff of Grumpy Old Men

Dale's Supermarket Sweep	ITV1	Contestant	1

Law of the Playground	Channel 4	Contributor	11

The Truth About Food	BBC 2	Contributor

2006–2007

QI	BBC 2	Panel member	4

1998–2007

Never Mind the Buzzcocks   BBC 2   Panel member
2

2006

Turn Back Time BBC 2   Interviewee 1

It's Funny Up North with... Vic Reeves   Tyne Tees   ITV1
Presenter

The Story of Light Entertainment   BBC 2
Contributor   2

Summer Exhibition   BBC 2   Panel judge

Comedy Connections – 'Shooting Stars' BBC 1   /Subject /
Interviewee   1

Jools Holland's Hootenanny   BBC 2   Interviewee
singer

2004–2006

Richard & Judy Channel 4   Interviewee   3

2002–2006

Friday Night with Jonathan Ross BBC 1   Interviewee 2

2005

The South Bank Show   ITV1   Subject / Interviewee   1

The Best & Worst of God   BBC 2   Presenter

Final Chance to Save   Sky One Contributor

Rogues Gallery Discovery Channel UK   Presenter   10

The Death of Celebrity   Channel 4   Contributor

50 Greatest Comedy Sketches   Channel 4   Contributor

2004

I'm a Celebrity... Get Me Out of Here!   ITV1
       Contestant (with Nancy Sorrell) 8

Who Do You Think You Are?   BBC 2   Subject
1

Star Sale   BBC 1   Contributor 1

Hell's Kitchen   ITV1   Boorish Customer   1

Breakfast   BBC 1   Interviewee 1

Vic's Chicks   BBC 3   Presenter   10   via the red
button

2003

Auction Man   BBC 1

Most Haunted   Living   TV   Celebrity guest (with Nancy
Sorrell)   1

2002

Celebrity Mastermind   BBC 2   Contestant   1   Reeves'
specialist subject was 'Pirates'

Surrealissimo – The Trial of Salvador Dalí   BBC 2

BBC Four   Paul Éluard

These Things Take Time – The Story of the Smiths
ITV1   Narrator

2001

It's Your New Year's Eve Party   BBC 1   Contributor

British Comedy Awards 2001   ITV1   Award presenter

I Love the '90s   BBC 2   Contributor   1   'I Love
1991' episode

We Know Where You Live. Live! Channel 4   Performer
        Four Yorkshiremen sketch

Comic Relief: Say Pants to Poverty   BBC 1 Presenter

Top Ten   Channel 4   Contributor   1   'Prog
Rock' episode

2000

Vic Reeves Examines   Play UK Presenter   12

Randall & Hopkirk (Deceased)   BBC 1   Marty Hopkirk
13

Robot Wars   BBC 2   Contestant

Night of a Thousand Shows   BBC 1

Dale's All Stars   BBC 1   Interviewee   1

This Is Your Life BBC 1 Episode for Tom Baker	Contributor	1	

1999

Clive Anderson All Talk	Channel 4	Interviewee	1

1996

TFI Friday	Channel 4	Interviewee	2

1995

Children in Need	BBC 1	Contributor

1993

British Comedy Awards 1993	ITV

Moir is a serious artist, as well as a comedian, although the two often combine, his works including paintings, ceramics, photographs and lino prints, being in a distinctive style. His work has been described as Dada-esque, surreal and sometimes macabre, his art and comedy having become different ways of expressing the same idea, James saying "I think putting your imagination on canvas or a television screen is the same thing, I don't differentiate between painting, acting or comedy. I think everything I do is art." Reeves has stated that he's an artist 1st, a comedian 2nd, hoping that he'll be remembered for his art and writing in 10 years' time, rather than his comedy.

Much like his comedy, Vic isn't one to analyse his artworks, having said that art should be "just for laughs", disliking folk looking for statements in his work, because there are none. "If something makes me laugh, that's it. I've done straight drawings and paintings ... but I haven't got as much pleasure out of them as if I'd done something that'd make me laugh". His work was described by artists Jake and Dinos Chapman as 'able to command our laughter as a purgative, to encourage the viewer to leak at both ends', artist Damien Hirst, a friend of Moir, having also described him as an influence.

The crossover of comedy and art often features within James & Bob's TV shows, as in The Smell of Reeves and Mortimer's first episode, in which several of Vic's drawings were featured, illustrating the lyrics of the opening song, later being published in his book 'Sun Boiled Onions'. As in the script book for the show, Moir often drew sketches for the BBC's costume and set designers saying that "if we just tell them what we want, it never ends up looking like it does in our minds".

Arts and crafts played a large part in James's upbringing, his mother, a seamstress, and father, a typesetter, made extra money by selling handmade wooden crafts and ceramics at local markets. Reeves began charging for his artistic services, including customising and painting his friend's school bags and elaborately embroidering clothing, later producing artworks his acquaintances liked, hoping that they'd buy them. Wanting to study art, but being pressured into getting a job, Vic began a 5-year engineering apprenticeship at a factory in Newton Aycliffe with the aim of working in their technical drawings department.

After completing the apprenticeship, Moir applied to Goldsmith's College in London to study art, failing to get a place but sneaking in to use their equipment. He completed a one-year foundation course at Sir John Cass College in 1983, where

James later became an honorary graduate. Once leaving college, he worked as a curator at the independent Garden Gallery in London, where he held his first art exhibition during 1985, with the help of a grant from Lewisham Council.

He's published two books of his art, Sun Boiled Onions (1999), followed by 'Vic Reeves' Vast Book of World Knowledge', in 2009. His drawings were also included in his autobiography Me:Moir Volume One, along with the published script book for The Smell of Reeves and Mortimer. He provided 30 illustrations for Random House's reprint of Jerome K. Jerome's classic story 'Three Men in a Boat' (2011). James was also commissioned to create several celebrity drawings for Jools Holland's Channel 5 series Name That Tune.

Vic has hosted several exhibitions of his artwork, including:

Sun Boiled Onions (2000) at the Percy Miller Gallery

Doings (2002) at the Whitechapel Gallery, London

My Family and Other Freaks (2007) at the Eyestorm Gallery, London

Where Eagles Tremble (2009) at Mews of Mayfair, London

Hot Valve Leak: Visual Ramblings of Vic Reeves (2013) at the Strand Gallery, London

A selection of Moir's paintings were displayed at the Saatchi Gallery, London during 2010, as part of an exhibition by charity 'The Art of Giving'. He was also a judge for the charity's open art competition.

James took part in the Illuminating York festival during 2012, his illuminations, named 'Wonderland', being projected across a number of historic buildings including the Yorkshire Museum, St Mary's Abbey, and the 10-acre site of York Museum Gardens.

Before becoming famous as a comedian, Reeves was a member of several bands with many different names and musical styles, in which he usually played bass guitar and/or sang. Vic sold tapes of his early material in the back pages of NME magazine under the name 'International Cod'. Mark Lamarr, later to become a team captain in Shooting Stars, was sent a tape of Moir's group 'Fan Tan Tiddly Span'. When James appeared on Never Mind the Buzzcocks in 1998, Lamarr repeatedly played a sample from the song 'Fantasia (Side A)' to embarrass him.

As part of early Big Night Out performances, Reeves would sometimes hand out promotional materials to the audience. On one occasion he handed out a 7" flexi disc of original song 'The Howlin' Wind'. Having surplus copies of the discs, Vic passed them on to Darlington-based band Dan who then included a copy of the disc with their L.P. Kicking Ass at T.J.'s.

'I Will Cure You', Moir's only album, was issued during 1991 by Island Records, hitting UK No. 16, having featured the chart-topping single 'Dizzy', which was a collaboration with The Wonder Stuff. It included a mixture of covers and original songs in a variety of musical styles, many of which were originally introduced in Big Night Out. A couple of other singles were also released from the L.P., a cover of the Matt Monro song 'Born Free' and a dance reworking of Christian hymn Abide With Me, which reached No. 6 and No. 47 in the UK Singles Chart, respectively.

James and Bob issued a cover of The Monkees song 'I'm a Believer' with British group EMF in 1995, which hit UK No. 3, Reeves having previously sung the track at the beginning of early Big Night Out performances in London, and opened the Channel 4 series with it. In the music video, which Vic directed, the duo dressed as Mike Nesmith and Davy Jones of The Monkees. On the CD release of the single, a studio version of 'At This Stage I Couldn't Say' was included, a track originally sung by characters Mulligan and O'Hare in The Smell of Reeves and Mortimer. On the 7" issue, the bonus track was 'At Least We've Got Our Guitars', which was the opening song for the last episode of The Smell of Reeves and Mortimer.

The theme to British stop-motion animation Shaun the Sheep, sung by Moir, was released as a single during April 2007, the song making UK No. 20. Reeves and Mortimer contributed backing vocals to Jools Holland's 'Holy Cow', a Lee Dorsey cover in 1990, the track being included on Holland's album World of his Own and also issued as a single. James later advertised Holland's L.P. Moving Out to the Country.

Vic provided backing vocals for Morrissey's cover of 'That's Entertainment' that year, originally by The Jam, his vocals not being used in the final edit but he was thanked (as Jim Moir) in the sleeve notes of Morrissey's 'Sing Your Life' single, which featured 'That's Entertainment' as a bonus track. A fan of the Smiths, Reeves opened some episodes of Big Night Out with covers of the band's songs, including 'Sheila Take a Bow', which he intended to include a cover of on his album I Will Cure You but it didn't make the final cut.

James contributed a track to Ruby Trax (1992), a compilation L.P. released by NME magazine to commemorate 40 years of the publication, having covered the Ultravox song 'Vienna', but drastically altered the original lyrics. Vic contributed to Twentieth-Century Blues: The Songs of Noel Coward (1998), a tribute album featuring artists including Elton John, Sting, Robbie Williams and Paul McCartney. Moir covered Coward's track 'Don't Put Your Daughter on the Stage Mrs. Worthington' (1934), which was arranged by David Arnold for the L.P. The song, described by Reeves as 'sinister', was initially recorded with all original verses intact, but as the last included foul language, it was edited out of the final issue.

James's cover of 'Ain't That a Kick in the Head?' was featured during the year 2000 as a bonus track on the theme single to the Randall and Hopkirk (Deceased) series in which he starred. Vic was originally due to duet with Nina Persson of the Cardigans, who provided vocals, but missed the final cut. A shortened version of Moir's cover also featured in the series, Reeves and Mortimer appearing in the music video for the single.

Jim has also appeared in music videos for other artists, his first having been that for Shakin' Stevens' single 'What Do You Want to Make Those Eyes at Me For (1987), being hired for the shoot for £10. Vic was also in the music video for Band of Holy Joy's song 'Tactless', the following year, introducing the group then appearing at the bar part way through. The video was filmed in Deptford, London, with original advertising posters for Big Night Out being seen at the beginning.

Vic Reeves' Vast Book of World Knowledge – a surreal encyclopaedia with text and artwork by Reeves. Atlantic Books, was published in October 2009. It followed Vic Reeves Me:Moir

(Volume One) – autobiography by Vic Reeves, Virgin Books, 2006 & Sunboiled Onions – diary, paintings and drawings by Vic Reeves, Penguin Books, 1999

James has appeared in TV adverts, both with Bob and alone, one for Guinness quoting Moir as saying "88.2% of statistics are made up on the spot". Vic has featured in solo advertising work for a variety of products including MFI, Müller Light, First Direct, Churchill Insurance, Cadbury's Boost, Mars Bar, Fanta, Heinz Tomato Ketchup, Domestos bleach and Maryland Cookies, having cross-dressed for an advert for 888 Holdings' Bingo website 888 Ladies in 2008.

Jim also advertised Jools Holland's album Moving Out to the Country during 2006. Reeves was in an East Coast Trains TV advert to promote the first-class service in 2011, having sketched then painted passengers and an attendant. Moir was also in a radio advert for the company the following year.

James Roderick Moir is the son of James Neill (1926–2004) and Audrey Moir (née Leigh). He moved from Leeds to Darlington, County Durham when 5 years old, with his parents and younger sister Lois. Jim attended Heathfield Infants and Junior School then went on to the nearby secondary school, Eastbourne Comprehensive in Darlington.

Vic has 4 children, the eldest two by his first wife Sarah Vincent, whom he wed during 1990 then divorced in 1999. He met his 2nd wife, Nancy Sorrell, during 2001, the couple marrying on 25th January 2003. Nancy gave birth to twin girls Beth and Nell at the William Harvey Hospital in Ashford, Kent, on 25th May 2006. Reeves lives in Charing, near Ashford, where he buried his classic Austin A40 Somerset car in his back garden, as shown on the Omnibus documentary 'A Film of Reeves & Mortimer', shown on the BBC during 1997. James & Bob are lifelong fans of the rock band Free.

"I came up with the Vic Reeves character for a stage project, folk presume that's my name, even when I do other acting jobs. I've been trying to shake it off for about 20 years. Vic started off as an overblown northern club compere, then slowly evolved into a complete idiot.

The first thing I remember – and this has been qualified by my mother – is being in a pram. She left me outside a shop and I remember seeing corrugated iron above me, so I was probably quite disturbed that she'd abandoned me. I also remember a kid called John Boxer, who locked me in his toy box.

My playground growing up was the fields and forests. I had a brief stint in London in my 20s, but I live in the country again now. I go walking and birdwatching. I've just finished a documentary about video arts, one of the films including a lot of wading birds on an estuary. I could name them all.

I've been accident-prone since I was a kid climbing trees and falling out. I've come off a few motorcycles. A few years ago, I went under a tractor. I've been under a lorry. The last time, I had a huge bruise on my left buttock, like a black plate, so I had to sit in a peculiar position. I tried to keep it quiet, but it was spotted one morning when I got out of bed.

Painting is my chief passion. I've always done it. I've just put a bit more effort into it over the past 10 years. It pays more money than other work for a start. I've got notebooks all round the house and I go into my studio at the end of my garden virtually every day. I'm still lively, 60 is like 40 now, isn't it? I've just finished a Big Night Out and I was leaping off the desk. I got famous in my 20s, so I kind of stick at that age.

I've got a 26-year-old, a 22-year-old and two 13-year-olds. The twins think I'm some ancient megalith. What I really like doing is surprising them by secretly studying things that make me look cool, like learning the Fortnite dance. I cook every day and find it really relaxing. I've got a huge number of cookery books. It's usually traditional British and French cooking, but then I'll go off-piste. I've just been doing Ainsley Harriott's Caribbean.

There's a lot to be depressed about, so I try to avoid doing it. The constantly hot summers are a bit of a worry and plastic. We were at a fish and chip restaurant recently, where they had sachets of vinegar. I found myself being a grumpy old man: "Look at all this plastic, why don't you just have the vinegar in a bottle?" I don't say it publicly, I just do my own private mithering. After my early youth of thinking isn't socialism fantastic, I let life pass by.

Vic and Bob were bringing their Big Night Out back to the BBC. The Christmas special, which was followed by a 4-part series, included a jaunty song about trousers, a skit on First Dates, a punch-up, Ed Sheeran, some 'observation comedy' and a baker from Wisconsin selling 'perfuffle' cakes. You should see the stuff that didn't make the edit, said Reeves. "There were some spectacular moments, like when we tried to get a horse on the stage". A horse? "We wanted to look under it and see what was going on, but the horse was a bit frisky. He wouldn't go on". Mortimer gestured at the BBC Comedy offices opposite. "You'd think there'd be someone out there who deals with horses".

It was 30 years since Jim Moir and Bob Mortimer teamed up, so when the BBC asked them for a one-off special, they'd decided to go back to their roots. Their first TV show, Vic Reeves' Big Night Out, a surreal spoof of a variety show, debuted on Channel 4 in 1990. James was Vic Reeves, the flamboyantly controlling compere; Bob was his sidekick, playing all manner of roles from The Man with the Stick to Morrissey the consumer monkey.

Vic and Bob's Big Night Out brought back some of that show's key elements - grumpy Graham Lister, bizarro talent segment, Novelty Island then the closing song, mixing it with a dash of The Smell of Reeves and Mortimer, along with a hint of Shooting Stars. Basically, it was half an hour of peculiar sketches, wigs, bickering and unsettling props. "Everyone's a one-trick pony aren't they?" said Bob. "It always ends up being the same ballpark. We've only ever done what we like. We do what we enjoy doing, because then it looks like you're enjoying yourself. We are enjoying ourselves", said Moir.

When they were writing, Mortimer drove from his house in Tunbridge Wells to Jim's near Ashford for 9.30am then they worked through until 2pm. "Just talking and shouting. We'll say, 'what shall we write a song about? Blackberries? Chinese parrots?' Then Jim says 'trousers' and we both laugh our heads off. Learn your lines, no autocue, no retakes. Just 3, 2, 1, go. It feels like a nice challenge. If you really, really are funny, you've got 30 minutes", said Bob.

When they shot the original Big Night Out, their scripts were 3 pages long, they wouldn't let the cameramen see them in advance, shooting the whole show in 30 minutes. "We got into trouble for it. We're not telly people. We didn't know the rules and naively we wanted everyone - the cameramen and so on - to laugh when they heard it on the night. We genuinely didn't want to give the jokes away," said Mortimer.

They wanted the new show to feel as immediate as in the old days, so they filmed it at the intimate Hospital Club in London, having hired Mat Whitecross, known for music documentaries including Oasis: Supersonic, "to shoot it live, like a pop concert". It took 50 mins from start to finish, whereas most TV comedy shows take hours. "It's dreary, innit. We guess that we're the only ones stupid enough, who have the balls? The balls, Jim?" asked Bob. "The gusto", corrected Vic. "The gusto, to do an underwritten show - go out in front of an audience and just film it. Learn your lines, no autocue, no retakes. Just 3, 2, 1, go. It feels like a nice challenge. If you really, really are funny, you've got 30 minutes".

It was an ethos that had served them well so far. Ever since Mortimer, then a solicitor, was one of 7 audience members at a comedy night in the Goldsmiths Tavern in New Cross, where he watched Reeves tap-dance in a Bryan Ferry mask with planks tied to his feet. A couple of weeks later, Moir got Bob up on stage then presented him with a giant cheque for £8m made out to 'ill kids'. They started writing together the next day.

Their success was stellar - their audience doubling by the week. "If you were going to see Jim, you were going back next week, but taking someone with you" said Bob. The show went from the room above the pub to the room downstairs, to the Albany Empire, where they were spotted by Alan Yentob and Michael Grade, who put them on Channel 4.

"The comedy circuit kind of resented us, because they were slogging away. We never fitted in anywhere - not by design, that's just what we thought was funny. We've never copied anyone else. Originally from having a lack of knowledge about what comics do then realising, we're onto a winner here, because no-one's doing anything like this. Now there are a lot of young lasses and lads and they're quite intense - there isn't that joy. They want to get on telly and on panel shows. Our motivation came from having a laugh. We're the only double act that is left," said Vic. Ant and Dec? "They're more like presenters. They just read off an autocue and someone writes it all". Mitchell and Webb? "They're just actors in some sketches. We've written and learned then we veer off. There's no-one at all doing that", said James.

The key to their success, said Mortimer, was that they got into comedy to have fun, rather than a career. "It was just a way of us having a nice night out. The route for two blokes in a pub in Deptford to being on telly didn't exist - maybe for Oxbridge types, but that wasn't the end game. "What do modern comedians do? Do they just tell long, rambling stories? And you occasionally get a laugh?" said Reeves. "It's the weirdest thing, Vic. I'm seeing some famous comics now who want to be gurus," marveled Bob.

They had absolutely zero interest in incorporating a message, or even a nod to current affairs, in their comedy. "I've never in my life met anyone as apolitical as Jim. I seem to remember on the day of the Brexit vote you weren't aware of it. I asked how you voted and you were like, 'What for?' It's not a bad place to be, really. We come from the school of if you're going to do comedy, we want to cram as many laughs as we can. One every 5 mins wouldn't do me. We want one every 5 secs", said Mortimer. "I'm only interested in fine art. We'd never put anything political in what we do, because I don't think it's the right thing to do", said Moir.

That was the rationale behind their bonkers sitcom House of Fools, which was axed by the BBC after two seasons during 2015. "We thought it was fabulous", said Bob. "We thought it was the pinnacle. We tried to get as many laughs in as possible. I think we probably would be in the Guinness Book of Records for the amount of laughs in a sitcom. The BBC say, 'It's got to have warmth, there's got to be a narrative, there's got to be a character like this, an enemy. We kind of ignored that and thought - surely five people can just say funny lines for 24 minutes. We had a bit of a story - there'd be a big moth attacking the town, or something. There aren't any decent sitcoms on now. I can't think of any," said James.

The pair went back on the road in 2016 for the first time in almost two decades. The tour was postponed for 3 months when Mortimer went for a routine check-up, discovering that his arteries were 95% blocked. He was booked in for a triple heart bypass 4 days later. On the morning of the operation, he thought he might die, so wed his long-term partner, Lisa, with whom he has two sons, aged 19 and 20.

Bob said he was fine now, being a lot less worried than he was soon after the operation when he lived off a diet of seeds. "Has your food regime changed? When we were on tour, he refused a pork pie from Melton Mowbray, which I thought was ridiculous. Would you have a pork pie now?" asked Reeves. "I eat all sorts of sh*t, Jim and you just feel bad. For people who've had heart operations, it's very difficult at the moment because half of science believes you shouldn't eat any saturated fat and half of science believes you should eat as much as you can. So you eat a cake, then you eat a statin, and think, 'that will work'", said Mortimer.

"You could do a modern stand-up routine about it," said Vic. "Yes, I'd go on at Edinburgh with me heart story. It'd all build up to me eating a pork pie on stage and everyone would be standing up, clapping, saying, 'yes that's rather clever'", said Bob. It was, said Moir, a shock to see his comedy partner so ill, having started getting chest pains in sympathy, patting his chest. "It's psychosomatic but you think, 'Oh God'. You get to a certain age..."

That week he'd been worried that he had emphysema. "I was a bit short of breath but then I found quite a lot of people had the same chest infection". He'd begun swimming half a mile / day, after dropping his daughters off at school. "I go early so there's me and a lot of old ladies. Old ladies everywhere". At the age of 58, did they worry about doing what they do and getting older? "Physically, yes, but we're still very spritely. I notice it when we're still writing things that would suggest we're about 30. We should be writing about widows, not 'Ooh I've got a new girlfriend'", said James.

Their reunion tour had been more sedate than their previous one during the '90s, when they'd drunk all night after shows - "ending up in some club in Liverpool then some council estate in Manchester...", said Mortimer. These days, they'd have a pint of the local real ale then go to bed. They didn't socialise as much as they'd used to, either, when they'd seen each other every night, gone on holiday together. "It's that family thing, you retreat to your house," said Bob. "I like making dinner and watching the telly," agreed Vic, who had 11-year old twins with his 2nd wife Nancy Sorrell and two older children from his first marriage.

In recent years, they'd worked on solo projects, Mortimer's surreal football podcast Athletico Mince having amassed over 7 million listens. Reeves painted most days in the huge studio that he'd built at home - he'd recently been creating screenprints of the original Big Night Out paintings. "Noel Fielding bought two of my paintings the other day," he said. "They're beautiful, Jim's paintings," said Bob, who had a painting Moir had done of him on his hospital bed with a heart pinned to his chest, with another of a large fluffy elephant. "You can keep that one", said James.

Thirty years on, their instinct was still - if it makes them laugh, it works. "If we make each other laugh then everyone else laughs," said Vic. "I went to a comedy show recently, which wasn't particularly funny but he was very engaging. I had this terrible feeling that his end game was to make people think, 'He's a thoughtful, clever bloke isn't he?' My hope is that people leave saying, 'that was funny, that was'", said Mortimer. "Or 'Those two are proper idiots. Pair of morons. Are they really that thick?'" agreed Reeves. "'They're complete f*cking idiots,'" said Bob, happily. "That's such a compliment". Strange fella...

'Have you ever damaged your phone in unusual circumstances? e.g: It's fallen on a very hard lizard or it's melted during prayer,' asked Mortimer. It turned out that Jim said there was an anal-based incident on a ridge which fitted the bill. Thereafter, further lines of questioning included: "Is it inappropriate to have a comforting funeral candle scented with bubblegum? On a cross-Channel ferry do you mainly stare at the funnel or the railings? Have you ever rented out a room for men to sleep? Have you ever been to Peterborough - on your own? Do you wish that Sports Direct sold food as well?

To that last question Moir replied "I'd love to have a sneaker which has an interior compartment, which contains hummus or taramasalata or any of the Greek dips". At a preview event in London to mark the return of their show to BBC Four, there was some insight into the pair's career of over 35-years, as they shared archive pictures – as well as some indiscreet celebrity gossip.

James recalled a certain future Britain's Got Talent judge loitering on set while they were shooting their sketches. "He used to hang around everywhere. You'd look in the corner and there was Walliams. It's because we got Matt Lucas on when he was 17, who said 'Can I bring my mate along?' He used to hang around in corners. One time – and I do remember this – when we were doing Randall & Hopkirk, we filmed a scene for an hour and a half then all of a sudden Walliams came out of a wardrobe. He'd been hiding in there. Very strange fella". "There's some truth in that," Bob added.

After being shown a photo of himself in Jools Holland's office in Greenwich, South London, where they used to write Big Night Out, Mortimer recalled: "We had an English Gentlemen's

Motorcycle club. You had to have an English motorcycle and dress like an English gentleman. Paul Young, the singer of 'Wherever I Lay My Hat', asked if he could join. He came in wearing those leather trousers with tassels all down the side". He drove a Harley-Davidson,' Vic added.

Bob continued: "Me, you and Jools went into a room while he waited outside – we decided he couldn't join". Reeves stated that they based their rules on the Hell's Angels initiation ceremony in which new members had to bite the head off a chicken: "Our rules were that you had to present a chicken dinner to every guest. Also, whenever you pass a lady you raise your helmet".

Mortimer recalled rather a bruising first encounter with the acting legend Derek Jacobi. "We were doing Randall and Hopkirk, I hadn't met met him. He was called something like let's say, Professor Whittingshield. They went, 'Action!' I said, 'Hello, Professor Whislingshield', getting it wrong. He went, 'Oh you c*nt!' – with the word intoned violently". Vic also recalled a scene from the same episode, when a hefty guard had to punch Bob, who was supposed to move out of the way but he didn't, so the actor knocked him unconscious 'For about 5 minutes'.

Reeves recalled a gruelling shoot with the former Dr Who in a studio that was a roasting 140F. "It was ridiculous, but Tom said, 'Jim at the end of this I'm going to make a Tom Baker Special'". Which turned out to be a gin and tonic or rather "It was a bucket full of gin and he threw a lemon in it. We actually drank it". The pair lived relatively close to each other in Kent, so Moir, a regular house guest, later bought Baker's house off him, although he didn't disclose whether it was bigger on the inside... Next to it was a churchyard, James recalling: "He already had his grave there, which said 'Tom Baker 1934-' ... but with no end date. He's the greatest bloke".

The audience at the event at the British Film Institute were shown several photos from Vic's own archive, including an early incarnation of the oddly attired character Tom Fun. "I'm going to say this is 1992. Those were fantastic days of wardrobe, with make-up staff who'd say, 'We don't know what you want to do, and you obviously don't, here's a big bag of stuff' then we'd come out looking like that developing the characters from that".

Another pic showed Moir on stage at the Regent's Park Open Air Theatre in London, with a badly-made puppet having the face of Nick Kamen, the model who was famous for a steamy ad for Levi's jeans set in a launderette in 1985. James recalled: "These puppets were made by me. As you can tell, not by an expert. This is long before the Big Night Out went on TV. I got commissioned – commissioned!

I got asked to do a concert in Regent's Park with Suzanne Vega. I turned up but they were horrible people. Suzanne Vega and all her crew were having a nice dinner. I came along then said 'I'm the warm-up turn'. They took me to what was pretty much a woodshed that had shovels in it, told me to wait. I said, 'Can I have a drink?' Someone gave me a can of lager when all the others were having this nice food". It was no better when Vic got to the stage, "They thought I was going to be a stand-up but it was a lot more than that. No one liked it; everyone hated every single moment".

That opinion was also shared by some reviewers, the pair sharing a write-up they received of a night in Malcolm Hardee's notorious Tunnel Club during the '80s, which described them as 'riotously unfunny'. It sarcastically described a sketch in which

30

'the area's least-gifted crab gave a lecture on the forests of Scotland. The audience was deeply impressed by this, clamouring for the next act but the Walker Brothers turned out to be pantomime bears leaping around to music. Their antics included a simulated sex act'.

Another picture showed Reeves as Tappy Lappy, a very early character from the days he performed Big Night Out at Goldsmiths Tavern in South London. Moir and his pal Johnny Irvine had cut out portraits of Bryan Ferry from the front of Face magazine, having taped them to their own heads, preempting the cardboard face masks that appeared in joke shops everywhere.

"Bob turned up that night to see Tappy Lappy. We sellotaped wooden planks to our feet, having had tap dancing sound effects made by dropping cutlery and cans in our house. Turning to his friend, he said: 'You saw that then thought, 'I want to be part of that'. Then Bob said: 'You'll never know, Jim'. It was amazing to come to that as a stranger and know there was nothing like that in the world". Thirty-five years on, there still wasn't...

32

42

BOB & VIC

71

81

Lightning Source UK Ltd.
Milton Keynes UK
UKHW020715290922
409643UK00009B/947